1 MONTH OF FREE READING

at

www.ForgottenBooks.com

By purchasing this book you are eligible for one month membership to ForgottenBooks.com, giving you unlimited access to our entire collection of over 700,000 titles via our web site and mobile apps.

To claim your free month visit: www.forgottenbooks.com/free106530

* Offer is valid for 45 days from date of purchase. Terms and conditions apply.

ISBN 978-0-484-13216-9
PIBN 10106530

This book is a reproduction of an important historical work. Forgotten Books uses state-of-the-art technology to digitally reconstruct the work, preserving the original format whilst repairing imperfections present in the aged copy. In rare cases, an imperfection in the original, such as a blemish or missing page, may be replicated in our edition. We do, however, repair the vast majority of imperfections successfully; any imperfections that remain are intentionally left to preserve the state of such historical works.

Forgotten Books is a registered trademark of FB &c Ltd.
Copyright © 2017 FB &c Ltd.
FB &c Ltd, Dalton House, 60 Windsor Avenue, London, SW19 2RR.
Company number 08720141. Registered in England and Wales.

For support please visit www.forgottenbooks.com

MEMORIAL

OF THE LATE

GEN. JAMES S. WADSWORTH,

DELIVERED BEFORE THE

New York State Agricultural Society,

AT THE CLOSE OF ITS

ANNUAL EXHIBITION AT ROCHESTER,

SEPTEMBER 23D, 1864,

By LEWIS F. ALLEN,

OF BUFFALO, (EX-PRESIDENT OF THE SOCIETY.)

ALBANY:
VAN BENTHUYSEN'S STEAM PRINTING HOUSE.

1865.

W13A

MEMORIAL.

Mr. President, Officers and Gentlemen
    of the New York State Agricultural Society:

WHEN good and great men die, it is the impulse of generous hearts, in unavailing regrets for their loss, to pay a fitting tribute to their private worth and public services. From time immemorial, States, communities and societies with which they have been connected, or to which they had rendered eminent benefits, have borne prompt and honorable testimony to their virtues and actions, not only as the expression of gratitude and respect to their memories, but to inspire posterity as well as their cotemporaries with an admiration of good deeds and beneficent labors. All worthy societies and associations have had inscribed on their member-rolls names of distinguished men and benefactors—and this Society, although humble in its pretensions, unambitious of worldly renown, and cultivating only the arts of peaceful life, may claim, not boastfully, but with heartfelt satisfaction, names most honorable in their efforts for human welfare, and deeply lamented in their too early departure from the field of their labors.

At a meeting of the Executive Committee of your Society in May last it was "*Resolved*, That a memorial of the late JAMES S. WADSWORTH, of his connections with this Society, with the agriculture of his county, and of the State, and his devotion to his country, be prepared and read before the Society at its annual exhibition in September next at Rochester."

In obedience to that resolution I come before you to speak of that lamented man, late a President of this Society. This rich and populous Valley of the Genesee was his home, and in and around it was the principal theatre of his action. His name was almost a household world throughout Western New York, and he was loved and honored by all who knew him. This is the place to speak of him, and of his connection with the agricultural interests of his county, of his vicinity, and of the State—of his labors in their behalf, and his influence on their welfare. Most gladly, yet respectfully, would I have preferred that this task should be discharged by one who more intimately knew, and better appreciated the life of this excellent man, than myself; but the duty placed upon me by the committee seemed imperative, and I responded to their command with great diffidence in my ability to do justice to the occasion. You will pardon what may, perhaps, seem a digression from the immediate subject of this memorial, but the scope of the "resolution" demands a more discursive notice of the agricultural events and progress of this vicinity than what have passed under our own immediate observation.

Seventy-four years ago, the spot on which we stand—this opulent and thriving city, ringing with the sounds of human industry—this broad and magnificent valley, reaching from the lake, almost within our sight, to the distant hills on the southern border of our State, was a wild, unbroken wilderness. The victorious army of General SULLIVAN, under the direction of our recently formed National Government, had just driven the predatory Indian bands from their forays on the border settlements of the Chemung, and Tioga, to their distant forest homes, and they gladly consented to bury their enmities, and live in peaceful intercourse with our people. The broad and fertile lands of Western New York had been purchased by various individuals and companies, both in the Eastern States and Europe, and were about to be laid open for settlement. In the year 1790 two young men, entrusted with agencies for the disposition of large tracts of these lands, left their homes in Connecticut, and after a journey of several weeks through formidable difficulties, a portion of the way clearing their forest road with axes, they gained the banks of the Genesee at Big Tree, thirty miles south of what is now Rochester. The name of these two young men was WADSWORTH. William, six years the elder, was a man of bold, determined temperament, vigorous, indomitable will, skilled in the stern and rugged arts of life, possessing the power to reduce the forest to culture, and imbued withal, with a military spirit, eminently fitting him as a pioneer in the great work which invited him to its achievement. James, the younger, was of a milder quality. He had been liberally educated. His mind, penetrating and expansive, had been highly cultivated, and his habits trained to business. System, order, and perseverance, were the rules of his action. Thus, with the extraordinary opportunities laid out before the brothers, success was sure to follow their undertakings.

In the discharge of their agencies they divided and sold extensive tracts of land, and invited a multitude of settlers into the Genesee Valley, and throughout its immediate borders. Industrious and thriving communities grew up, and teeming fields with bounteous harvests opened and ripened all around them. Possessing the love of domain, inberent in their English ancestry, the WADSWORTHS, as they progressed, invested their earnings in choice tracts of the rich valley, until their acres were counted by thousands, and in process of years "the Wadsworth farms" became famous, not only in the country round about, but in the old settlements of Eastern New York and New England. William was the out-door man and farmer; the forests fell, and the fields were cleared under his sturdy perseverance: while James was the office-man and financier; and it was mainly his fine rural taste and wise forecast, aided by the vigorous thought and industry of his brother, which gave outline to their estates and system to their agriculture. Great herds of cattle fattened in their meadows; numerous flocks of sheep ranged their pastures; and over their wide uplands the richest wheat ripened for the sickle and the reaper. Even in those early years they sought improved breeds of horses, cattle, sheep and swine, and introduced them to their farms, and by their example gave tone and impulse to a style of husbandry among the farmers around them, which has been continued to the present day.

Time wore on. The pioneers of the Genesee country, one after another, were gathered to their fathers, and WILLIAM WADSWORTH, a bachelor, in the year 1833, at the age of seventy-one years, bearing an honorable record as a general officer in the militia of his county, at the memorable battle of Queenstown, on the Niagara frontier, in the war of 1812, and of a life marked by useful labors at home, went down to his grave, bequeathing his share of the Wadsworth estates to his brother and his children.

JAMES WADSWORTH had married at middle age, and established his family home on the spot of his first settlement, then become a neat and thriving village, called Geneseo. Here were born and reared his children, two sons and three daughters, not one of whom is now living. Thriving in his fortunes, cultivated in his tastes, and accomplished with the advantages of foreign travel during some years' residence in Europe, where the business of his agencies had early called him, he became widely known for his genial hospitality, his diguified manners, and his elevated intercourse with society. Few country gentlemen in the United States—none, certainly, in the State of New York—through their wide business correspondence abroad and at home, were better or more favorably known. His plans of improvement were broad, comprehensive and thoroughly practical. Much of the grand beauty and park-like scenery of the Genesee Valley owe their effect to his refined taste and æsthetic judgment. He patronized education by donations for the improvement of our common school system, and gave liberally for school and town libraries in his county. He maintained the systematic plans of agricultural routine adopted by his brother and himself at an early day, and as circumstances required, improved them. After a life of temperance, frugality and usefulness, in the year 1844, at the age of seventy-six years, he died, leaving his family, probably, the finest agricultural estate in the country.

A historical allusion to the Wadsworths', and their farms, forty-five years ago, may contrast that early day in the Genesee Valley with the present. I find the narrative given in a letter from the late celebrated Dr. THOMAS COOPER, then of Pennsylvania, dated May 21, 1809, while on a tour through Western New York. It was published in *The Port Folio* in the year 1810. He is describing the Home Farm of the Wadsworths:

"Col. W. WADSWORTH, who is unmarried, lives with his brother, Mr. JAMES WADSWORTH. The particulars of this noble farm are briefly as follows: The house (a double house of five windows in front, with good-sized rooms) is placed on an eminence at the farther end of the village of Cheneseo, which contains about a dozen houses. There is a gentle descent of cleared land in front of the house for about three-quarters of a mile, to the edge of the flats. The flats are a mile and a quarter across. Of these, full in view from the windows of the house, Col. Wadsworth and his brother own 1700 acres, all cleared and laid down in timothy and clover. Besides these 1700 acres of flats, they have three or four hundred acres of cleared upland in front and around the house. Their present stock is twelve hundred sheep, with between six and seven hundred lambs; of these lambs sixty-eight are half-blood Merinoes, and two hundred half-bred Bakewell's. They purchased a full-blooded Merino ram from Chancellor LIVINGSTON, out of the (French) Emperor's flock at Rambouillet.

Messrs. Wadsworth also keep on the same farm two hundred mules. The mules they import young from Connecticut, improve them here, and send them, when full grown, to the Southern States, where they fetch from sixty to one hundred and twenty dollars apiece. They have also a stud of forty horses. On this tract they have three dairies, let out on shares. They furnish each tenant with a house and buildings, and with forty cows. The tenant takes care of the buildings, cuts the grass for hay, and retains half the butter and cheese. On a farm farther down the river they have about two hundred and thirty head of horned cattle. They complain of want of capital to stock the land fully.

"Mr. James Wadsworth has arranged a very well-chosen library of about six hundred volumes of the best modern books; doubtless the best room in this neat and well-furnished house. The establishment in all its parts seems to give a full and favorable picture of that truly respectable character, an active, intelligent, industrious gentleman farmer.

"*They have no land of their own on the flats for sale. What they possess the family mean to retain.*"

JAMES SAMUEL WADSWORTH, whose recent sudden and melancholy death we now mourn, was the eldest son of JAMES WADSWORTH, and born in the town of Geneseo, in the county of Livingston, in the year 1807. Endowed with a robust physical constitution, coupled with a bright and vigorous intellect, he was educated, not in the pent-up schools of a crowded city, but as all country boys should be, in the best schools of a country village. His collegiate course was completed at Harvard University. He afterwards acquired the profession of the law, partially in the office of DANIEL WEBSTER, in Boston, and finished his course of law reading in Albany. Born to the inheritance of great wealth, accomplished in education, professional knowledge, and the advantages of elevated society, on arriving at his majority the most flattering allurements to personal ambition, to luxury, and worldly enjoyment, so dazzling to the imagination of a spirited young man, were spread before him. But young WADSWORTH was both thoughtful and considerate. Though loving, and reasonably indulging in the pleasures of society, he calmly surveyed his position at the outset of what might become an important life. His uncle William, the out-door manager of the landed property of the family, was in the sere and yellow leaf of declining age. His father, bowed with forty years of toil and responsibility, had looked hopefully to a time of repose, and James, with a manly resolution, and thorough appreciation of his duty, threw aside the blandishments of fortune, turned his attention to business, and gradually assumed the chief supervision of the family estates. In the year 1833, at the age of twenty-six, Mr. WADSWORTH married the daughter of JOHN WHARTON, Esq., of Philadelphia, a lady of great personal worth, and a connection every way eligible to their mutual happiness. He established his family home at Geneseo, and erected his dwelling with attachments and surroundings comporting to his condition of estate, and range of life and occupation. There in the midst of congenial society, and the interchange of those amenities which flow in the familiar intercourse of friends and neighbors, he lived, and labored, and dispensed a widely participated hospitality. Of his family, Mrs. WADSWORTH, and six children—three sons and three daughters survive him.

Probably no agricultural property in the country, so extensive in domain, had been arranged into a better division of individual farms, and their husbandry directed with more systematic economy on the part of the landlords, than those of the Wadsworths. The soils were applied to those crops most congenial to their natures, and which yielded the most profit on their outlay; and as proof that the mutual interests of landlord and tenant were thoroughly studied, I understand that quite three-fourths in number of the tenants now on the farms are those, and the descendants of those, who occupied them in the lifetime of the elder Wadsworths.

In noticing the management of an overshadowing agricultural estate like this, a remark might be expected upon the tendency of such extraordinary holdings, and their influence upon the welfare of those who rely on them for support. Such discussion is hardly germane to this occasion; yet I frankly admit, that the system of aggregating land in large bodies by individual proprietors, and holding it under a tenant cultivation, has not generally proved favorable to the highest prosperity of the communities connected with them. The system is scarcely in accordance with the spirit of our Republican institutions. In this instance, however, it is a gratifying fact that the moral and pecuniary condition of the inhabitants dwelling on the Wadsworth farms is as high, and the line of husbandry has been as good, in the average, as among the smaller farmers who hold their lands in fee—and the general agriculture of Livingston county is of no mean order. Nor can any sensible man throw merited censure upon the conduct of the elder Wadsworths in thus amassing, and holding with tenacious grip, such a noble domain. In the vigor of their young manhood they went into a wild country, and grappled with all the hardships and diseases incident to a reduction of the broad wilderness to life and civilization. Improving their fortunate advantage, they won their possessions fairly. God had made the land beautiful in its undulating surface, and blessed it with surpassing fertility. Magnificent landscapes of wood, and meadow, and swelling upland; of crystal lakes, and leaping streams, and flowing river stretched far and wide around them a land most goodly to behold; and with ready eye and sagacious plan they saw, possessed, and enjoyed it. And they used it well.

In the year 1841, by an act of our Legislature, the State Agricultural Society was reorganized. Through an appropriation from the State treasury its funds were augmented, and an exhibition of farm products and mechanical implements was ventured. Under the new administration of its affairs, the first exhibition was held at Syracuse, in September of that year, and with such degree of success that its annual repetition was demanded. In January, 1842, JAMES S. WADSWORTH, of Geneseo, was unanimously elected president of the Society. For several years he had pursued the business of a farmer on his own account, as well as supervised the chief agricultural affairs of his father's estate, and in his own vicinity was known and esteemed as a thrifty, intelligent husbandman. It was fit and proper that such an one as he should receive the honor and take the responsibility of the office. The Society, although successful, so far as its imperfect organization in a new field of exertion had proved, was yet to be further systematized and put in working order. With characteristic energy, Mr. Wadsworth entered upon the discharge of his duties, and the good conduct and well-doing of the Society enlisted his heartiest attention. He became, at the same time with his father and brother, a life member, and, with the aid of his spirited associates in office, placed it on a sure basis of success. The next exhibition was at Albany, and a most gratifying display of improved husbandry, household art, and mechanical skill was offered to the congregrated and expectant friends of our agricultural advancement. The degree of tact, aptitude and readiness in the discharge of his duties evinced by the young president, determined the Society to re-elect him, and appoint the exhibition for the year 1843 in the city of Rochester, the vicinity of his home, where his attention could be readily given to its preparation. And most amply was that preparation made. His personal services and ready purse were both yielded for the occasion. The Genesee Valley poured forth the choicest of its agricultural abundance, and the skill and handicraft of the young and active city joined in their rival display, while the more distant country, east and west, met each other with their mutual offerings. This, the third exhibition of the Society, larger in material and more numerous in attendance than either of the two which preceded it, was but the growth of well directed effort on the part of its managers and the increasing spirit of the people. The career of the Society was no longer a probation; and, assured of its success, Mr. WADSWORTH, at the close of his official term, with well won honors, gracefully retired to give room to his successor.

The death of his father during the succeeding year threw the management of three-fourths of the Wadsworth estates—that portion belonging to himself and sisters—upon James, the other fourth being owned and managed by his younger brother, William. Not only the lands in the Genesee Valley, but other extensive real and personal properties had come to his charge, and he addressed himself to their care with an industry, an ability, and a knowledge of their multifarious interests quite equal to the necessity. He maintained the system of management which had been long adopted, and had only to extend it over such routine and details as became necessary by changes or aggregations incident to such extended affairs. He continued his labors both in the councils and at the annual exhibitions of the Society, and for many years his farm stock formed a prominent feature in the prize lists. On all occasions he evinced the liveliest interest in its welfare; and, as soon as he had a son old enough—and his second one he trained to be a farmer—the stripling appeared among us with his fatted bullocks, and blooded horses, in honest competition with the hardest-handed farmer in the show grounds.

Nor were the agricultural efforts of Mr. WADSWORTH confined to the State Society. He took an active interest in his own County Association, and vigorously assisted its efforts in improving the husbandry of his vicinity. He imported from abroad choice breeds of farm stock, and in various manner promoted the welfare of the farmers of Livingston by his own example, as well as by his aid in the encouragement of new and economical inventions in labor-saving implements. His influence, always active, was persistent and beneficial throughout.

More intimate with the varied interests which build up the prosperity of the community outside of agriculture than the elder Wadsworths had been, James became engaged in several of the active enterprises with which the business men of Western New York were identified. He embarked a share of his capital in them, and gave to these different investments a portion of his attention. Nor in these was he merely a fair-weather adventurer. In important enterprises with others, he took risks, and heavy ones when his judgment approved, shirking no responsibilities upon those less able to bear them, but breasted such emergencies as in the hazards of business might arise, and by the further aid of his capital or credit, when necessary, brought to a successful issue their undertakings. He was emphatically a man of the times—a part and parcel of the entire community in what concerned their material welfare, and no man among them all was more alive to the prosperity of the people, aside from purely selfish motives, than himself. Enjoying the well earned returns of intelligent enterprise, and improving, by a liberal participation with others, the fortunes of himself and his family, his action redounded largely to the public good.

An incident may here be related testifying to the esteem and affection in which Mr. WADSWORTH was held in the community where he lived, and was best known. In December, 1851, business having called him to Europe, he took passage in the steamship Atlantic on his homeward voyage. The vessel did not arrive in New York at the expected time. Some days afterward a report came that she had met with an accident at sea which might prove fatal to her safety, and so long was further intelligence delayed, that by many the ship was given up for lost. It was known that he was on board, and during twenty-eight days of weary suspense, thousands of subdued voices and anxious hearts outside the agonized circle of his own fireside, testified their sorrow at his probable fate. His loss would have been felt as a public calamity. But a joyous day ere long shone out on both kindred and friends. Intelligence of his arrival in New York was speeded over the wires, and a day or two later he was welcomed to his home in Geneseo by the sound of bells and the congratulations of his assembled friends and neighbors.

In public affairs the opinion and action of Mr. WADSWORTH were decided. He took a lively interest in the leading questions of the day—not the lower issues affecting mere party politics—but questions involving grave principles, and policies worthy the attention of statesmen and philanthropists, in which his views were thoroughly defined, and inflexibly determined. Had he sought civil promotion, it was always open to his acceptance; but the tranquil paths of private life were more congenial to his tastes and feelings.

But a new and untried field of action was suddenly destined to open before him. Early in the year 1861 the atrocious rebellion in the Slave States of the Union against the general government, found him at his temporary residence in the city of New York. The President of the United States had called for troops to defend the seat of government from spoliation, and possible capture at the hands of the rebels. The national treasury robbed; the navy sent abroad and scattered in distant seas; the army—what there was of it—dispersed along our wide-spread frontier, and the material of defence squandered or carried away by the parricidal hands of a recently expired administration who had sworn in all solemnity to support the Constitution of their country; in this hour of its extremity, Mr. WADSWORTH, in the impulsive patriotism of his nature, rushed to that country's rescue. With his own purse and credit he furnished a vessel with a cargo of army supplies, went with it to Annapolis, and gave his personal attention to its distribution among the troops which had been hastily called to protect the city of Washington. This assistance on the part of Mr. WADSWORTH, so timely rendered in the impoverished condition of the public treasury, although afterwards repaid to him, was none the less creditable to both his patriotism and liberality. He then offered his services to the government in any capacity where they could become useful or important, and from that time forward abandoned his private affairs to the care of his agents, and devoted his entire energies to his country. As a volunteer Aid to General MCDOWELL, he engaged in the first battle of Bull Run, and by his courage and energy, retrieved much of the disaster of that ill-fated engagement. In July, 1861, appointed a Brigadier General, he was assigned to a command in the army of the Potomac. In the succeeding month of March, he was ordered to Washington, as Military Governor of the city, and for nine months discharged with distinguished ability the duties of that difficult and important post. In December, 1862, at his own request, he was ordered to the field. He reported to Major General REYNOLDS, commanding the First Corps, and was assigned by that distinguished officer to the command of his First Division, and afterwards led that division in the battles of Fredericksburg and Chancellorsville. At the battle of Gettysburg his was the first division engaged, going into action at nine o'clock in the morning, and fighting until four in the afternoon, encountering the severest part of the action, and suffering the heaviest loss of any portion of the army. Our troops winning the battle, and routing the enemy from the field, General WADS-

WORTH, comprehending the vast consequences depending on the immediate subjugation or capture of the rebel forces, urged the commanding General, MEADE, to their pursuit. But in vain. Other and more timid counsels prevailed, and that invading host of rebels was suffered to escape with the mild punishment of a simple defeat. The daring courage and stern energy of General WADSWORTH, on this decisive field, placed him, in all the high qualities of a soldier, second to no other general officer in the army.

Nor was he, of his family, alone in his devotion to the public service. Two sons followed him into the army. The elder one, Charles, was attached to the Department of the Gulf—served as captain under General BANKS, and participated in the attack on Port Hudson. With a year of active service, at the call of imperative duties at home, he resigned his command. The younger son, Craig, was attached to General WADSWORTH's staff for a time, and afterwards held responsible and hazardous positions with other general officers in various departments, until May last, when important domestic duties called him home. The son-in-law of General WADSWORTH, Capt. RITCHIE, also joined the army early in the war. He was engaged in General BURNSIDE's first expedition, afterwards served in the several battles at Port Hudson, and continued in active service until the melancholy event of the Wilderness compelled his resignation. If, in the annals of time, an instance of higher patriotism and intenser devotion to the honor of their country has been shown by a father and three sons, possessing millions of wealth, and beckoned by all the allurements of ease and luxury from personal danger, that instance has yet to be written; and would that the narrative of hard fought battles and bloody sacrifice would stop here.

General WADSWORTH took an active part in the arrangements and preparations of the campaign of General GRANT in the spring of 1864 against the rebel army in Virginia. His judgment in council and energy in action had placed him in such estimation with the military authorities, that, at the outset of the campaign, he was charged with a leading command. A decisive work was before the army of the Potomac. The country had become impatient of delay in its long anticipated advance, and anxiously expectant of better results than had, in the past, marked its checkered fortunes. This feeling was known to no one better than to WADSWORTH. He responded to it with all the fervor of his unfaltering nature, and with a determination, on his own part, that it should not be disappointed. The incidents attending the opening of the campaign and its first battle of the Wilderness, so melancholy in its results, are of such interest that I shall be excused for laying some of them before you, which I obtained from Captain CRAIG W. WADSWORTH, a son of the General, who was in a part of the battle:

"When the army of the Potomac was reorganized last spring, my father was placed in command of the fourth division, fifth corps. This division was made up of his old division of the first corps, with the addition of another, the third brigade. He crossed the Rapidan on the 4th of May. On the evening of the 5th his command was engaged for several hours, and lost heavily. On the morning of the 6th he was ordered to report to General HANCOCK, commanding the second corps, and by him was ordered into action on the right of that corps. My father made several charges with his division, and finally carried quite an important position, but was unable to hold it, the enemy coming down in superior numbers. This was about eight o'clock A. M., the fighting having commenced at daylight. About this time General HANCOCK sent for my father, and told him he had ordered three brigades, Generals WARD's, WEBB's, and one from General BURNSIDE's corps, to report to him, and he wished him, if possible, with the six brigades under his command, to carry a certain position. Three or four assaults were made without success, the fighting being terrific. My father had two horses killed under him. General HANCOCK then sent word to my father not to make any further attempts to dislodge the enemy at present. This was about eleven o'clock A. M. The enemy did not show any further disposition to attack. It was HILL's corps which my father had been fighting. Everything remained quiet until about twelve o'clock, when LONGSTREET precipitated his corps on my father's left, and hurled back WARD's brigade at that point, in some confusion. My father, seeing this, immediately threw his second line, composed of his own division, forward, and formed it on the plank road, at right angles to his original line, the ditch at the side of the road affording his men some protection. It was in trying to hold this line, with his own gallant division, then reduced to about sixteen hundred men, that he fell. His third horse was killed that morning, about the time he was wounded. The enemy was charging at the time, and got possession of the ground before my father could be removed. He was carried back to one of the rebel hospitals that Friday afternoon, and lived until Sunday morning."

To illustrate somewhat the carnage of war and its uncertainties, I may relate the whereabouts of the son, Captain CRAIG WADSWORTH, at "The Wilderness" battle: "During the 5th and 6th of May, the division of cavalry to which I was attached, was guarding the wagon train. On the morning of the 6th, I obtained permission from my General, TORBERT, to go up to the front, and remain two or three hours with my father. I reached him between eight and nine o'clock, and remained with him until he received the order from General HANCOCK not to make any further attempt to dislodge the enemy. I got word about this time that General TORBERT was moving, so I rejoined my command. We started out with General SHERIDAN on his raid, the next morning, and I never knew positively of my father's death until we reached the White House."

This narrative will scarcely be complete without the letter of PATRICK MCCRACKEN, to the widow of General WADSWORTH, a copy of which has been kindly furnished me. It reads as follows:

SPOTSYLVANIA COURT HOUSE, VA.,
May 9th, 1864.

Mrs. General Wadsworth, New York:

Dear Madam—You have heard, before this reaches you, of the death of your brave husband, General WADSWORTH. I saw him in the hospital, near the battle-field, on Saturday last, about ten o'clock; he could not speak or take any notice to anything; he held a paper in his hand with his name and address written on it; he was surrounded with the most eminent surgeons in the Confederacy, who done everything for him that could be done; one of them took the paper out of his hand, and when he laid the paper back against his hand, he opened his hand and took it back again; he did not seem to suffer much, the ball had entered the top, or rather the back of his head. I saw him again on Sunday, about nine o'clock. I had carried some sweet milk to the hospital, and wet his lips several times, and let a little go down his mouth. But when the surgeon raised him up, he could not get him to let any go down. When I returned to the hospital, about three o'clock, he was dead and in a box ready for interment. I told the surgeon in charge that I was a prisoner nine weeks in the Old Capitol, while the General was Military Governor of Washington, and that I would have a coffin made for him, and bury him in a family burying ground; he cheerfully consented. After much trouble, I had a coffin made for him, as good as any could be made in the country. When I went for his remains with the coffin, General LEE had given special orders, (not knowing I was going to take charge of his remains,) that he should be buried by a large tree, the tree to be cut low, and his name marked on it. I had given the surgeon satisfactory evidence that I would take care of the body, and with the advice of Captain Z. B. ADAMS, Co. F, 56th Mass. Regt., they gave me the body. I removed it from the box to the coffin, and brought it home last night, and buried it this morning in the family burying ground at my house; he is buried with all his clothing, as he fell on the battle-field. The grave is dug with a vault or chamber, the coffin covered with plank, and then dirt. When arrangements are made by our government for his removal, I will take pleasure in having him moved through our lines to his friends. I live about a mile to the left of the plank road, as you go from Fredericksburg to Orange Court House, near New Hope Meeting House, on the plank road, twenty miles from Fredericksburg and eighteen from Orange Court House.

*   *   *   *   *   *   *

I had a large plank planed and marked for a headstone, and placed it at the head of the grave. He received all the attention and kindness at the hands of the Confederate authorities that could be bestowed upon him, as will be attested by Captain Z. B. ADAMS, Co. F, 56th Mass. Regiment.

With great respect, I remain yours,
PATRICK McCRACKEN.

Thus, on the soil of his country's foe, far from the soothing hand of sympathy, or the loved embraces of those he held most dear—his brain shattered—his mind unconscious, but a glorious memory awaiting him—died, and was temporarily buried, this noble, generous soldier. Though slain upon a distant battle-field, his remains now rest in the burial ground of his native village. The hand of filial affection rescued them from a profaned grave. They were tenderly removed, and, under the escort of a detachment of Invalid Corps, from Washington, arrived at Geneseo on the morning of the 21st of May, after a lapse of fifteen days from the time he fell, and were deposited within the walls, and amid the heart-stricken circle of his now desolated home. A multitude from the surrounding and even distant country, had come to meet the arrival of the Dead Soldier, and pay their last tribute of respect at his grave. His burial was simple, as was fitting to his grand and simple life. In the afternoon of the day, the remains were removed to the Episcopal church of the village. The solemn ritual of his own Christian faith was said, and then, preceded by a veteran corps of the 21st Volunteer Regiment, from Buffalo—one of the earliest which entered the war, and himself had led to battle—and followed by a great concourse of those who had long loved, and now mourned him, his body was borne to its final rest.

> "And there he sleeps till at the Trump Divine,
> The Earth and Ocean render up their dead."

It may appear superfluous to speak further of General WADSWORTH, or to delineate his character to those who knew him so well as you; but to those who did not know him—and his fame is the property of his country—it is but just to speak of him as he deserved. An allusion might be made to the more matured policy and opinions which influenced him, beyond mere impulse, to enter into the military service of his country; but this is not the time, nor is it the place, for such allusion. The graver and more deliberate pen of history will do justice to both, when it shall write the full measure of his intentions and contemplated action, had his life been spared to disclose them. That they were wise and beneficent, as they were entirely unselfish—reaching far beyond any aspiration to mere military fame or the applause accorded to temporary success—is known to those who were intimate with his thoughts.

To a friend who carelessly asked him one day, why, with so much to care for at home, he sought the hazards of the battle-field, he nobly replied, that "they who had the most at stake should not shrink from the heaviest risks for their country's safety!"

He was not ambitious of political distinction, as shown by his declining the office of Governor of the State, some years ago, when his simple assent to the wishes of his party friends, then in a powerful majority, would have elected him. Nor did he aspire to high military command. At the breaking out of the rebellion, he magnanimously urged upon the President of the United States the appointment of General Dix to the office of Major General, on account of his greater military experience and fitness, although a political opponent, when they had both been named by the Executive of New York for that position, and under the rule of the War Department, at Washington, but one of them could be accepted.

He did, indeed, discharge one civil deliberative trust, but that scarce a legally official one. He attended, with several other delegates from the State of New York, in February, 1861, the so-called "Peace Congress," at Washington, in an effort to adjust the sectional difficulties between the Free and Slave States, just preceding the rebellion. But with the chronic traitors of the South, in that body, he could have no affiliations. He could yield no rights which he knew the Free States to possess under the Constitution; nor would he admit the arrogant pretensions of the South to privileges for slavery which the Constitution had not given them. No one sustained the integrity and honor of the Northern States with more firmness or decision than WADSWORTH; and, after exhausting all honorable efforts on the part of the Northern delegates in composing, without success, their differences, the congress adjourned, and he, with his associates, withdrew to their several homes. He had also previously, in the year 1856, discharged the duty of a Presidential Elector for the State at large; and again, in 1860, that of an Elector for his own congressional district, to which offices he was severally elected by the people.

To an intimate friend of General WADSWORTH, (the Hon. DANIEL H. FITZHUGH, of Geneseo,) I am indebted for some relations of his private life which I have given you, and in addition I repeat some of his words:

"I have known General WADSWORTH since he was a boy of ten years old, and his early years gave promise of what his manhood would be. Although never quarrelsome, he was always ready to resent insult, or resist oppression. His friendships were fixed and unwavering, and to serve a friend, he would risk to any extent either person or property. His domestic relations were most happy. A more kind, indulgent, or affectionate husband and father, I have never known. His hospitality was unbounded, and as a host, I have met with few who possessed so happy a faculty of entertaining their guests; his conversation always animated, amusing and instructive. He lived a truly Christian life, although not a professor of religion. He loved his fellow-men, and was always foremost when any charity was to be dispensed, or any project was on foot for enlightening, elevating, or benefiting, in any way, the human family. He was liberal to his tenants, in the abatement of rents, when their crops had been destroyed, or injured by insects, floods or droughts. Brave to rashness, he was generous, liberal, humane. Highly intelligent and well educated, he possessed all the qualities which make men good and great. In short, I have seldom known an instance where so many high qualities have been combined in one individual, and would to God we had more like him in this trying crisis of our country!"

Such is the testimony of one who knew him for nearly fifty years. In a personal acquaintance with General WADSWORTH for more than thirty years, I have seldom or never known one for whom I had a greater respect. You all knew his athletic person, his cheerful look, his welcome greeting—and, if I may speak of so small a thing, his plainness of dress, the absence of bodily decoration, and utter disregard of personal trifles—yet always mindful of conventional proprieties; there was no nonsense about him. His bearing was manly, his words sincere, his sentiments outspoken. He was direct and cordial in manner, genial in his associations, affable to all with whom he had intercourse, irrespective of rank, or condition in life, yet decided in opinion, and frank in its expression. If any quality of his mind stood out conspicuously, it was that of a vigorous common sense, coupled with a ready judgment, applied to all matters which arrested his attention. This was manifested in various public questions which agitated the community, as well as in the management of the large estates, both real and personal, under his control, not only to the benefit of the estates themselves, but to the welfare of the communities with which they were connected. In all his business relations, I have never heard of an act of injustice or oppression at his hands. On the other hand, I knew him to pay an obligation of more than twenty thousand dollars which he had unwarily incurred, to assist a friend, and afterwards became void by its own tenor. It was uncollectable, and he knew it; and the party to whom it was given—a rich man—would be no real sufferer by its non-payment. But Mr. WADSWORTH, declining to avail himself of the illegality, or incur an imputation on his honor, paid the amount and submitted to the loss.

His faithfulness to the duties of any kind which he had undertaken, was a striking feature of his character. In the three years of his connection with the war, he did not altogether spend eight weeks of time at his family home. His soul was in his country's service. Nor was his attention alone absorbed in the simple official duties of the Commander. In camp, he was among his soldiers, in tent or in hospital, looking after their wants, ministering to their comfort, promoting their welfare, and correcting abuses where they existed—thus adding to the efficiency of his corps by every exercise of humanity, as well as by the sterner demands of the field. No General was ever more beloved by his troops than he.

Those who recollect the Irish dearth, of the year 1847, when the famished cry of millions of down-trodden sufferers reached America, will not forget the merciful bounty with which he contributed to freight a ship with corn, and gratuitously sent it out for distribution to the hunger-stricken people. Nor was he vaunting in his charities, timely and liberal as they were. It was characteristic of his benevolence to do good by stealth, rather than to be seen of men. He demeaned himself as one of the great human brotherhood, and I might even speak of his expression of indignant commiseration over the victims of a boasted "domestic institution," as in their crouching helplessness, side by side, he and myself, some years ago, stood over them at a human chattel market in one of the "chivalrous" Southern States. He had little respect for wealth, simply, or the hoarded gains of those who were altogether absorbed in its accumulation; and he respected just as little mere moneygetters. Manhood, character, liberality, and patriotic impulse, accompanied with their wealth—or those qualities without it—were the passports to his confidence and esteem.

His tastes were elevated and liberal. He esteemed his wealth less for his own pleasure, than for the benefit and happiness of others. He indulged in no idle display of luxury, yet the elegancies of life and the adornments of art found in him an appreciating admirer and patron. He promoted education and literature by frequent gifts, and left eight thousand dollars to erect a building for a town library and museum in Geneseo. His ruling taste was for rich lands, and their development to the prosperity and wealth of the country. He loved the soil in all its breadth of vegetable or mineral production. He loved to talk of agriculture, and its advancement—of crops, and their improved modes of cultivation—of horses and of cattle. He loved the broad landscapes of his native valley, the grand old trees in his ancestral meadows, and every natural and artificial thing which beautified the earth, and ministered to the benefit of man.

In remarking upon the wealth of General WADSWORTH, it may possibly be inferred that undue merit has been given him for the accident of its possession. Not so. It was not because he had wealth, but because he knew how to use his wealth, that I speak of him in terms of approbation. I strive to measure him the man he was. In this age of lax education, irregular habits, and impulsive action—an age in which money is the God of most men's adoration—he had wealth enough to spoil twenty common men, and it was a rare merit in him that with all the tempting opportunities at his hand, he withstood their fascinations. The wonder is that he was not a profligate, or—a miser.

But the last great labor of his life—his devotion to a country which he loved beyond all else—proved the virtue that was in him. Possessed of all that could render life enjoyable—friends, fortune, domestic love, and the consciousness of duty well discharged—he abandoned them all at the coming of his country's danger, went forth to its rescue—and, if might be, to die for its deliverance. He could equally well, as men would say, have served his country in contributing of his treasure to its necessities, instead of leading its soldiers to battle, and his valuable life been spared to his family, to the community and to the State. But such was not his own sense of duty, and his blood has paid the sacrifice of his devotion. In his death we, as a Society, mourn a friend and associate; the community in which he lived, a useful citizen; the State, an enlightened patriot; the army, a heroic soldier; and the nation a man worthy of its noblest honors. A life of active duty, crowned with achievements of loftiest intent, has written him high in the roll of illustrious men—the peer of any other in the annals of his time. Sleep! hero—patriot—benefactor! Peacefully sleep in your honored grave! And may that Almighty Power, who holds the destiny of nations in His hand, lift your beloved country from its present calamity, and redeemed from all servile oppression and bloodguiltiness, establish it a monument of righteousness to the world!

On the conclusion of the memorial, the Honorable Ex-Gov. JOHN A. KING (ex-president of the Society), offered the following resolution:

Resolved, As the sense of the members of the Society, that the death of our lamented associate and friend, JAMES S. WADSWORTH, fills our hearts with unfeigned regret and sorrow—that his absence from our deliberations and exhibitions is felt and acknowledged by all who knew his worth and intelligence. He was no common man. Liberally educated, with a sound, firm and discriminating mind; inheriting the broad lands of an honored father, the cultivation and management of which was his delight and occupation, he stood forth a noble example of an American citizen in all his relations. Foremost in the cultivation of the arts of peace, he gave his life in the defence of the Union and the Constitution of his country, when rebel hands were raised against them. Honored, therefore, be the memory of such a man, whose life and death were alike distinguished and glorious, and whose name must ever be a household word among the free homes of his native State.

The resolution was unanimously adopted.